DEBUGGING DECODED: THE 10 RULES GUIDE TO MASTERING CODE CHALLENGES

Contents

Presentation

Welcome to the "Troubleshooting: 10 Standards Guide." Investigating is a fundamental expertise for each developer, and dominating it can altogether improve your capacity to make powerful and productive programming. This guide is intended to give you a deliberate way to deal with troubleshooting, offering ten crucial principles that will help you analyze and fix issues in your code really.

1.1 The Purpose of Debugging

Acquiring an understanding of the significance of debugging lays the groundwork for implementing efficient debugging techniques. In this part, we'll investigate the job of troubleshooting in the product advancement process and its effect on the nature of your code.

1.2 Significance of Powerful Investigating

Not all investigating approaches are made equivalent. We'll examine the reason why powerful troubleshooting matters and how it adds to quicker advancement cycles, further developed code practicality, and generally project achievement.

Whether you're a fledgling software engineer or an accomplished designer, this guide will furnish you with significant bits of knowledge and noteworthy systems to handle bugs with certainty. We should plunge into the ten guidelines that will change your troubleshooting abilities and make you a more capable coder.

1.1 Reason for Investigating

Troubleshooting is a basic cycle in programming improvement that includes distinguishing, segregating, and fixing mistakes or bugs in a program's source code. The main role of investigating is to guarantee the smooth and blunder free execution of a product application. We should dig into the vital parts of the reason for investigating:

Identifying Errors The primary objective of debugging is to locate code errors or unexpected behaviors. This incorporates punctuation mistakes, coherent blunders, and runtime blunders that can prompt issues like accidents or wrong result.

Isolating Problems After errors have been identified, the problem areas need to be isolated. This includes reducing the extent of the issue, recognizing the particular parts or segments of code answerable for the blunder, and understanding the underlying driver.

Further developing Code Quality
Troubleshooting adds to generally code quality. By settling mistakes and refining the code, designers can make more hearty, proficient, and viable programming. Troubleshooting isn't just about fixing issues yet in addition about improving the general nature of the codebase.

1.2 Significance of Powerful Troubleshooting

While investigating is a typical practice, the viability of the troubleshooting system can fluctuate fundamentally. In order for software developers to produce high-quality software and maximize their productivity, it is essential to comprehend the significance of efficient debugging practices. Here's the reason compelling troubleshooting matters:

Time and Asset Productivity
Compelling troubleshooting saves time and assets by smoothing out the recognizable proof and goal of issues. Engineers can rapidly find and fix issues, lessening the investigating cycle and speeding up the advancement interaction.

Improved Code Maintainability
Code that has been well-debugged is simpler to maintain. By methodically tending to and settling issues, engineers make a more steady and viable codebase. This is especially important for projects that will last a long time and require constant upkeep.

Further developed Programming Unwavering quality
Compelling troubleshooting adds to the general unwavering quality of programming. By killing bugs, designers guarantee that the product proceeds as expected, giving a positive client experience and limiting the gamble of surprising disappointments.

We will look at ten rules that are the foundation of effective debugging practices in the following sections, giving you the confidence and precision to tackle coding problems.

Rule 1: Grasp the Code

Understanding the code is the first and central rule of viable investigating. Understanding the codebase's structure, logic, and flow is crucial before attempting any issues. Rule 1 focuses on two important aspects: Using code documentation and reading code efficiently

2.1 Effectively Reading

Code Overview Reading code effectively is a skill that distinguishes effective debuggers from the rest. This is the way you can improve this ability:

Code Design
Understanding the general design of the code helps in exploring through records and modules consistently. Perceive the

fundamental parts, works, and classes to acquire a significant level viewpoint.

Control Stream

Break down the control stream of the program. Identify structures with branches, conditionals, and loops. This understanding is pivotal for following the execution way and finding likely issues.

Variable Use

Inspect how factors are proclaimed, introduced, and altered all through the code. Focus on information types, scopes, and the lifetime of factors.

Modularization

Assess how the code is modularized. Efficient and measured code is more straightforward to fathom. Determine the roles that each module or function plays.

2.2 Code Documentation

Reason for Documentation
Documentation fills in as an aide for engineers to grasp the code's usefulness, use, and plan. Compelling documentation improves cooperation and helps in troubleshooting endeavors.

Remarks
Significant remarks give bits of knowledge into the reasoning behind code choices, calculations utilized, and expected entanglements. Survey remarks to acquire a more profound comprehension of the code.

The purpose, parameters, and return values of functions and methods should be documented. Developers will find it much simpler to use and troubleshoot code if there is clear documentation.

Programming interface Documentation

On the off chance that the code includes outer libraries or APIs, allude to their documentation. Understanding how to associate with outer parts is imperative for powerful troubleshooting.

By complying with Rule 1 and concentrating on fathoming the codebase, you establish a strong starting point for effective investigating. In the accompanying areas, we will investigate extra principles that expand upon this comprehension, outfitting you with the abilities expected to certainly explore and investigate code.

2.1 Effectively Reading Code

Overview Reading code effectively is an essential developer skill. It includes figuring out the grammar as well as getting a handle on the fundamental rationale and plan decisions. Effective methods for reading code include the following:

Code Construction

Module Recognizable proof: Perceive the fundamental modules, classes, and works in the codebase. This gives a significant level comprehension of the program's engineering.

Record Association: Comprehend how records are coordinated. Distinguish header documents, source records, and any design documents that might be available.

Control Flow Execution Flow: Follow the progression of execution through the code. Recognize circles, conditionals, and any leaps between various pieces of the program.

Problem Solving: Keep an eye on how mistakes are handled. For diagnosing unanticipated behaviors, it is essential to comprehend error-handling mechanisms.

Variable Utilization

Variable Lifecycle: Examine the usage of variables throughout the code. Comprehend where factors are pronounced, how they are instated, and where they are changed.

Information Types: Observe the information types utilized in factors. Conflicting utilization of information types can prompt unobtrusive bugs.

Modularization

Capability and Class Liabilities: Figure out the obligations of each capability or class. Modularized code is more obvious and keep up with.

Reliance Investigation: Recognize conditions between various modules or parts. This is vital for understanding what changes in a single piece of the code might mean for other people.

2.2 Code Documentation The Purpose of Communication Through Documentation: Documentation fills in for of correspondence among designers.

It conveys the reason, plan, and utilization of code.

Onboarding: The onboarding of new team members is facilitated by code that is well-documented. The learning curve for comprehending existing code is decreased by clear documentation.

Comments That Mean Something: Commentaries that shed light on the logic or reasoning behind particular code decisions should be written and read. Stay away from excess remarks and spotlight on making sense of non-clear parts.

Tasks and FIXMEs: Observe any Tasks or FIXMEs in the code. These remarks frequently feature regions that require consideration, improvement, or further examination.

Capability and Strategy Documentation

Capability Reason: Archive the reason for each capability or technique. Incorporate data about boundaries, return values, and any aftereffects.

Utilization Models: Useful usage examples should show how to call functions or methods. This assists engineers with utilizing the code accurately.

Programming interface Documentation

Outer Conditions: On the off chance that the code depends on outside libraries or APIs, allude to their documentation. Understanding how to associate with outer parts is fundamental for compelling troubleshooting.

By consolidating viable code perusing rehearses with intensive documentation, you set up for fruitful troubleshooting. Rule 2 builds on this by talking about how important it is to reproduce the problem in a systematic way.

Rule 3: Use Troubleshooting Instruments

Troubleshooting apparatuses are fundamental for recognizing, breaking down, and fixing issues in your code. Rule 3 stresses the significance of utilizing both implicit and outsider troubleshooting instruments to improve your investigating abilities.

3.1 Underlying Troubleshooting Apparatuses

Coordinated Advancement Climate (IDE) Elements

Breakpoints: Set breakpoints in your code to stop execution at explicit places. At runtime, you can examine variables and evaluate expressions thanks to this.

Step Inside the Code: Utilize bit by bit execution to figure out the progression of your program. Step into, over, or out of capabilities to pinpoint issues.

Watch Windows: Screen the upsides of factors continuously utilizing watch windows. This gives bits of knowledge into how factors change during execution.

Call Stack: To comprehend the sequence of function calls that led to the current point in your code, examine the call stack.

Logging

Print Proclamations: Decisively place print explanations in your code to yield variable qualities or messages. This is a straightforward yet successful method for following the execution stream.

Logging Libraries: Use logging libraries to make itemized logs with various log levels. Logging is particularly important for long-running applications and conveyed frameworks.

Profilers for Performance Profiling from Third Parties: Recognize bottlenecks and execution issues in your code utilizing profiling devices. Profilers give definite bits of knowledge into the time taken by various capabilities.

Memory Profilers: Recognize memory spills and wasteful memory use with memory profiling devices. This is significant for keeping up with the security of your application.

Intelligent Investigating

Intelligent Investigating Apparatuses: Investigate devices that offer intuitive troubleshooting abilities, permitting you to change variable qualities or execute code during investigating meetings.

Debugger Augmentations: Check for expansions or modules that upgrade the troubleshooting highlights of your IDE. These augmentations can give extra bits of knowledge and functionalities.

Static Investigation Apparatuses

Code Linters: Use linters to perform static investigation of your code, recognizing possible issues before runtime. This proactive methodology can forestall normal bugs.

Analyzers for Code Complexity: Break down the intricacy of your code with devices that recognize regions that might be inclined to mistakes or challenging to keep up with.

In conclusion, becoming an effective debugger necessitates adopting debugging tools. Whether you depend on worked in elements of your IDE or coordinate outsider apparatuses into your work process, dominating these devices will altogether upgrade your capacity to analyze and determine issues in your code.

4.1 Inherent Troubleshooting Devices

Implicit troubleshooting apparatuses given by coordinated improvement conditions (IDEs) assume a pivotal part in aiding designers distinguish and determine issues in their code. Getting to know these instruments can essentially improve your troubleshooting proficiency.

Incorporated Advancement Climate (IDE) Elements

Breakpoints

Setting Breakpoints: Place breakpoints in your code to stop execution at explicit lines. This permits you to examine the condition of factors and the program's stream at that specific point.

Contingent Breakpoints: Set breakpoints to set off just when explicit circumstances are met. This is valuable for zeroing in on specific situations or code ways.

Step Through Code

Step Into, Over, and Out: Explore through your code bit by bit. " Step into" permits you to enter capabilities, "Step over" advances to the following line in the ongoing capability, and "Step out" moves out of the ongoing capability.

Go to the Cursor: Execute the code until it arrives at the line where the cursor is situated, staying away from the requirement for inordinate venturing through.

Watch Windows

Variable Examination: Monitor the values of variables in real time with watch windows. This sheds light on the ways in which your program's variables shift.

Articulation Assessment: Analyze expressions in watch windows to comprehend complicated conditions and quickly calculate values.

Call Stack

Follow Capability Calls: To comprehend the sequence of function calls that led to the current point in your code, examine the call stack. This distinguishes the setting of the issue.

Explore Through Stack Casings: Go all over the call stack to investigate factors and code at various levels of the call order.

4.2 Third-Party Debugging

Tools While the built-in tools are effective, third-party debugging tools provide specialized features and additional functions to meet specific debugging requirements.

Profilers

Execution Profilers: Perform execution time profiling on a variety of functions to locate performance bottlenecks. Profilers give an itemized breakdown of where most of the time is spent.

Memory Profilers: Identify memory spills and dissect memory use examples to guarantee productive memory the board in your application.

Intelligent Troubleshooting

Information Control: Data manipulation tools for use in debugging sessions When experimenting with various inputs, this can be especially helpful.

Dynamic Code Execution: Debuggers that empower you to execute code pieces or change variable qualities intelligently while the program is stopped.

Static Investigation Apparatuses

Code Linters: Perform static examination of your code to distinguish potential issues, for example, linguistic structure blunders, code style infringement, or normal programming botches.

Analyzers for Code Complexity: Evaluate the intricacy of your code to recognize regions that might be trying to keep up with or inclined to blunders.

Joint effort Apparatuses

Remote Investigating: Apparatuses that work with troubleshooting in distant conditions, empowering you to investigate issues on servers or gadgets.

Monitoring Errors: Stages that track mistakes and special cases progressively, giving bits of knowledge into issues that happen underway.

End

Joining the capacities of underlying and outsider investigating instruments engages designers to handle an extensive variety of troubleshooting difficulties. The following principle, Rule 4: Start with Simple Tests, which builds on these debugging tools and emphasizes a methodical approach to problem-solving, is a good place to start.

Rule 4: Begin with Basic Tests

Beginning with basic tests is an essential way to deal with troubleshooting that permits you to distinguish and separate issues in your code efficiently. Rule 4 accentuates the significance of separating complex issues into sensible parts through the most common way of confining the issue and building viable experiments.

5.1 Secluding the Issue

Partition and Overcome

Breakdown the Code: Partition your code into more modest areas or modules. Center around each part in turn, making it simpler to distinguish explicit issues.

Remark Out Code: Briefly remark out segments of code that are not straightforwardly connected with the thought issue. This helps slender down the extent of examination.

Distinguish Reproducible Situations Repeat the Issue: Guarantee that the issue can be reliably imitated. Tracking and testing potential solutions is made simpler as a result of this.

Distinguish Explicit Sources of info: Disconnect the data sources or conditions that trigger the issue. Effective debugging requires a thorough understanding of the specific scenarios that led to the issue.

5.2 Structure Experiments

Make Negligible Reproducible Models

Improve on Experiments: Create minimal test cases that are focused on reproducing the problem. Eliminate pointless intricacy to really disconnect the issue.

Utilize Mock Information: If pertinent, utilize mock information or reproduce conditions that trigger the issue. This permits you to control the contributions during testing.

Cases on the Cover Edge Examine Boundary Conditions: Test your code with inputs at the lower and furthest restrictions of OK qualities. This distinguishes issues connected with limit conditions.

Think about Mistake Situations: Make experiments that purposely conjure blunder conditions. This guarantees that your code will gracefully handle exceptions.

Test Steadily

Begin with Fundamental Usefulness: Guarantee that the essential usefulness of the code is functioning true to form. Steadily present intricacy through gradual testing.

Confirm Every Change: Subsequent to making changes to the code, re-run the tests to confirm that the alterations address the issue without presenting new issues.

End

Beginning with basic tests is an efficient methodology that permits you to separate complex issues into sensible parts. By detaching the issue and building viable experiments, you make a strong starting point for the troubleshooting system. Rule 5: Check for Normal Missteps develops this establishment, directing you to recognize and address normal mistakes in your code.

Rule 5: Check for Common Errors

One important part of debugging is looking for common errors. Rule 5 spotlights on recognizing and tending to two sorts of normal mixups: grammatical and logical errors.

6.1 Syntax Error Messages

Review Code Syntax Inspect Focus on compiler or mediator blunder messages. They frequently give signs about the area and nature of punctuation mistakes.

Check for brackets and punctuation: Check that all enclosures, supports, sections, and other accentuation marks are utilized accurately. Confounded or missing sections can prompt language structure blunders.

Use Code Linters

Design Linters: Coordinate code linters into your improvement climate. Linters consequently look at your code for language structure blunders and give constant input.

Address Ideas: Notice linter ideas for code style enhancements. Settling language structure issues early can forestall more mind boggling issues.

6.2 Legitimate Mistakes

Examine Code Rationale

Audit Calculation and Rationale: Analyze the rationale and algorithmic progression of your code. Check to see that the order of operations corresponds to the intended outcome.

Follow Variable Qualities: Use investigating instruments to follow the upsides of factors during runtime. Recognize errors among expected and genuine qualities.

Unit Testing
Compose Unit Tests: Execute unit tests for individual capabilities or parts. Experiments ought to cover a scope of contributions to approve the rightness of the rationale.

Mechanize Testing: Set up computerized testing structures to routinely execute unit tests. Computerization guarantees constant approval as your codebase develops.

Peer Audit
Team up with Friends: Participate in code audits with associates. New points of view can assist with spotting legitimate mistakes that

might be neglected by the first engineer.

Match Programming: Consider pair programming meetings, where two designers cooperate. This cooperative methodology can prompt the distinguishing proof of sensible imperfections.

End

Checking for normal slip-ups, including grammar blunders and intelligent mistakes, is a basic part of viable troubleshooting. By resolving these issues from the get-go in the advancement cycle, you lay the preparation for steady and solid code. Rule 6: Decipher the Code into Segments expands on this establishment, directing you to efficiently move toward the investigating system by isolating your code into reasonable areas.

Rule 6: Segment the Code

Strategically segmenting the code into sections makes the debugging process easier. Rule 6 supporters for a "Separation and Win" procedure, permitting you to zero in on sensible segments of your code and deliberately troubleshoot each part in turn.

7.1 Separation and Vanquish Approach

Recognize Code Segments

Modularization: Figure out down your code into measured areas in light of usefulness. Every module ought to have a distinct reason and obligations.

Works and Classes: Recognize works or classes that exemplify explicit highlights or undertakings. This makes it more straightforward to separate and resolve issues inside a clear cut setting.

Detach Pertinent Code
Remark or Briefly Handicap Code: Use remarks or restrictive checks to separate explicit segments of your code. This assists you with reducing the concentration to the piece of the code where the issue is thought.

Make units that can be tested: Guarantee that each detached segment is a testable unit. In order to facilitate focused testing, it ought to have distinct inputs and outputs.

7.2 Troubleshooting a Section

at a Time Establish Strategic Breakpoints: Place breakpoints toward the start and end of the part you are investigating. You can see how variables were before and after that section was done because of this.

Contingent Breakpoints: Utilize contingent breakpoints to stop execution when explicit circumstances are met. This is particularly valuable for troubleshooting a specific part of your code.

Make Use of Tools for Debugging Step Through Code: Utilize the bit by bit execution component of your debugger to navigate through the detached segment. This aides in figuring out the stream and recognizing any disparities.

Assess Factors: Consistently examine the upsides of factors during investigating. Guarantee that factors are holding the normal qualities inside the disengaged segment.

Iterative Methodology

Roll out Gradual Improvements: Assuming that you recognize an issue, make little and gradual changes to the disconnected segment. Test the adjusted segment iteratively to notice the effect of each change.

Check Changes: In the wake of altering the code, rerun your experiments to check that the progressions address the recognized issue without presenting new issues.

End

Figuring out the code into segments and embracing a "Separation and Prevail" move toward works on the investigating system, making it more reasonable and deliberate. Rule 7: Print Troubleshooting develops this approach, directing you on viable ways of involving print articulations and logging for the purpose of investigating.

Rule 7: Print Troubleshooting

Print investigating is a commonsense and frequently viable technique for investigating code. Rule 7 spotlights on utilizing print articulations and logging techniques to acquire bits of knowledge into the execution stream, variable qualities, and possible issues inside your code.

8.1 Successful Utilization of Print Explanations

Key Arrangement

Recognize Central issues: Place print explanations at central issues in your code, like the start and end of capabilities, circles, or restrictive proclamations.

Print Variable Qualities: Yield the upsides of applicable factors to comprehend how they change during the execution of your code.

Contingent Printing
Troubleshooting Conditions: Use print proclamations inside restrictive blocks to confirm whether explicit circumstances are being met.

Iterative Result: In circles, print values at every cycle to follow how the circle advances and distinguish issues inside the circle body.

Print Statements with Descriptive Messages for Debugging Information: Remember graphic directives for your print explanations to give setting about the motivation of the result.

Timestamps: Consolidate timestamps into print articulations to follow the planning of occasions, particularly in lengthy running cycles.

8.2 Logging Methodologies

Logging Levels

Utilize Different Log Levels: Carry out logging with different levels like Data, Troubleshoot, Cautioning, and Blunder. This permits you to control the verbosity of the result.

Particular Logging: Use logging levels to empower or handicap various sorts of result in view of the seriousness of issues specifically.

Logging to Files Logging to Files: Divert log result to petition for long-running cycles or server applications. This empowers you to survey logs even after the application has finished execution.

Turning Logs: Log rotation can be used to control the size of log files. This forestalls log records from turning out to be too enormous and consuming unreasonable stockpiling.

Brought together Logging
Brought together Logging Administrations: Use brought together logging administrations or stages for disseminated frameworks. This permits you to total logs from various hotspots for far reaching investigation.

Log Investigation Instruments: Investigate log examination instruments that give highlights like pursuit, sifting, and perception to figure out huge volumes of log information.

Blunder Taking care of
Blunder Logging: Set up specific logs for exceptions and errors. Incorporate applicable data, for example, stack follows and setting to help with diagnosing and settling issues.

Alarms and Notices: Set up cautions or notices for basic mistakes, guaranteeing ideal consciousness of issues that require quick consideration.

End
Print troubleshooting, when utilized decisively with print explanations and logging, gives important experiences into your code's way of behaving. Rule 8

makes way for Rule 9: Collaborate and Seek Help emphasizes the significance of working in a group and utilizing other people's expertise during the debugging process.

Rule 8: Work together and Look for Help

Working together with colleagues and looking for help from online networks are strong systems for conquering testing troubleshooting situations. Rule 8 urges designers to embrace cooperation and tap into the aggregate information on the more extensive programming local area.

9.1 Group Joint effort

Code Audits

Customary Code Audits: Lay out a culture of standard code surveys inside your group. Peer surveys give open doors to new viewpoints and catch gives right off the bat in the improvement cycle.

Helpful Input: Empower helpful criticism during code audits.

Engineers can share experiences, recognize expected issues, and recommend elective methodologies.

Match Programming
Match Programming Meetings: Take part in pair programming meetings where two engineers cooperate on a similar piece of code. This cooperative methodology frequently prompts speedier issue ID.

Information Move: Match programming works with information move inside the group. Junior engineers can gain from experienced colleagues, and bits of knowledge from different encounters add to powerful arrangements.

9.2 Internet based Networks and Gatherings

Designer People group

Take part in Discussions: Join online designer networks and gatherings applicable to your programming language or innovation stack. Stages like Stack Flood, Reddit, and specific discussions give spaces to seeking clarification on some pressing issues and sharing information.

Add to Conversations: Answer questions and share your experiences to actively participate in discussions. Your reputation will rise as a result of your involvement in the community, as will your connections to other developers.

Collaboration in Open Source
Contribute to Open Source:

Participate in open source projects. Teaming up on open source programming opens you to various coding styles, best practices, and different critical thinking draws near.

Discourses in the Issue Tracker: Take part in conversations on issue trackers of open source projects. This permits you to look for help, report messes with, and team up with engineers around the world.

Platforms for Learning Online Learning Platforms: Stages like GitHub, GitLab, and Bitbucket give spaces to joint effort. Utilize these stages to share code, team up on projects, and gain from others.

Communities of interest: Participate in learning communities associated with your framework or programming language. These people group frequently arrange occasions, online courses, and mentorship programs.

End

Working together with your group and looking for help from the more extensive programming local area are necessary parts of viable investigating. Rule 9: Gain from Mix-ups expands on this cooperative attitude, directing engineers to think about their encounters, persistently learn, and further develop their troubleshooting abilities.

Rule 9: Learn from Mistakes

Growing proficient as a developer and debugger necessitates learning from mistakes. After resolving issues, Rule 9 emphasizes the significance of conducting post-mortem analyses and maintaining a mindset of continuous learning.

10.1 After death Examination

Recognize Underlying drivers

Underlying driver Examination: Lead an intensive examination to distinguish the main drivers of the issues you've experienced. Learn why the issue arose and how it was resolved.

Report Discoveries: Record your discoveries from the after death investigation. This documentation fills in as a source of perspective for future critical thinking and information sharing inside your group.

Share Bits of knowledge
Group Interviewing: Share your bits of knowledge with your group through interviewing meetings. Talk about the difficulties confronted, the troubleshooting procedures applied, and the illustrations learned.

Information Sharing: Add to inner documentation by sharing your encounters and arrangements. This helps fabricate an aggregate comprehension of normal issues and their goals.

10.2 Ceaseless Learning
Ponder Encounters

Intelligent Practice: Consistently consider your troubleshooting encounters. Consider what functioned admirably and what could be gotten to the next level. Utilize this self-appraisal to refine your troubleshooting approach.

Observe Victories: Recognize effective troubleshooting endeavors, both independently and collectively. Commending victories builds up sure propensities and lifts the general mood.

Remain Refreshed
Ceaseless Training: Remain informed about refreshes in programming dialects, systems, and apparatuses. Persistent instruction guarantees that you are furnished with the most recent information and troubleshooting methods.

Peruse Contextual analyses: Investigate contextual analyses of testing troubleshooting situations. Gaining from the encounters of others expands how you might interpret assorted critical thinking draws near.

Try different things with Instruments and Strategies

Attempt New Apparatuses: Try out new methods and tools for debugging. A few devices might be more qualified for explicit situations, and investigating them improves your toolbox.

Code Difficulties: Take part in tasks and challenges related to coding. These exercises give potential chances to work on troubleshooting in a controlled climate and further develop your critical thinking abilities.

End

Gaining from botches is a continuous interaction that adds to individual and expert development. Rule 10: Test the Fix guides developers through the process of conducting systematic tests of their solutions to ensure the code's long-term stability and builds on the concept of continuous improvement.

Rule 10: The final step in the debugging process is to test the fix

To make sure that the problems that were found have been effectively fixed without causing new problems. Rule 10 instructs developers on how to create test cases for the fix and conduct regression testing to verify the code's stability.

11.1 Making Experiments for the Fix

Confine the Fix

Make Confined Experiments: Foster experiments that explicitly focus on the issue you recognized and fixed. By isolating the tests, the fix can be confirmed to solve the issue.

Extreme Cases: Incorporate edge cases in your test suite to guarantee the fix handles limit conditions. This is essential for affirming that the arrangement is strong across different situations.

Test Various Situations
Duplicate Unique Issue: Check to see if your test cases can replicate the problem. This is a basic move toward affirming that the fix really resolves the issue.

Negative Testing: Test the fix against situations that recently caused the issue. Check that the issue no longer happens under these circumstances.

Assess Effect
Influence on Other Usefulness: Think about how the change might affect other parts of the code. Run tests on related usefulness to affirm

that the fix doesn't present new issues somewhere else.

Execution Testing: Assuming the fix includes execution enhancements or changes, lead execution testing to guarantee that the general framework execution isn't adversely impacted.

11.2 Relapse Testing

Complete Testing

Run Full Test Suite: Execute your whole test suite, including both new and existing experiments. Relapse testing guarantees that the fix doesn't unintentionally break already working usefulness.

Mechanized Relapse Tests: On the off chance that conceivable, mechanize your relapse tests to smooth out the testing system and work with ordinary testing during improvement.

Variant Control Coordination
Joining with Rendition Control: Incorporate your testing interaction with form control frameworks. This permits you to run relapse tests consequently at whatever point changes are pushed to the code storehouse.

Consistent Combination (CI) Pipelines: Integrate relapse testing into your CI pipelines. CI frameworks can consequently run tests when code changes are made, getting potential relapses early.

Screen for Oddities
Mistake Checking: Set up blunder checking devices to recognize oddities underway. Ceaseless

observing distinguishes any unforeseen issues that might have fallen through testing.

Client Criticism: After the fix has been deployed, pay attention to user feedback. Effectively look for input from clients to get issues that might not have been distinguished during testing.

End

Testing the fix is a basic move toward the troubleshooting system, guaranteeing that the recognized issues are settled without presenting new issues. By methodically making experiments for the fix and performing relapse testing, designers add to the general solidness and dependability of their codebase.

This finishes up the "Troubleshooting: Guide to 10 Rules." Recall that troubleshooting is a constant educational experience, and each investigating experience gives a chance to refine your abilities and approaches.